# AYE BRO, YOU BE F*CKIN' WITH STOCKS?

## THE STRAIGHT-UP GUIDE TO OWNERSHIP, WEALTH, AND LEARNING THE MONEY GAME

ISBN: 979-8-9995483-0-6 (Paperback)

# | DEDICATION

To the boy who sat in that 8th grade classroom in 2008 and wrote,
"CEO of a Fortune 500 company"
under the question: *"Where do you see yourself in 10 years?"*

You had all the ambition in the world—but no map.
It's taken longer than we planned, but I never forgot you.
Every step I take is to honor your dream.
That untouched soul.
That pure fire.
That unshaken vision.

I'm still carrying you. And we're still on the way.

# | FORWARD

"*Aye Bro, You Be F*ckin' With Stocks?*" is a question. Not the type you ask a financial advisor, nor a tax professional, but a question you ask your homie, your *brother*.

This book is the answer to that question. It's not a lecture or a sermon. It's a real-life working guide for YOU to get started in the stock market. Something to cut through the noise and the red tape.

But why should you listen to me?

Well, just like you, I didn't grow up talking about stocks. I didn't grow up hearing about Roth IRAs, index funds, or generational wealth. I grew up hearing about bills. About saving. Holding on to every dollar you had. Put it under your mattress. Work hard, keep your head down, don't rock the boat—and in 30 years, maybe you'll retire and live comfortably.

Investing? That was for the rich. For white people.

Money was stress, yet money was everything.
Money was survival—yet the lack of it was death itself.
And anything beyond that? Fantasy.

But I knew that couldn't be the whole story.

At some point, I got exposed to something I—statistically speaking—wasn't supposed to see. A glimpse into a different world. A world where money moved differently. Where people didn't just earn, they grew. They flipped, they scaled, they passed it on. And from that moment on, I realized the game was bigger than just working hard. It was about ownership. Leverage. Access. It was about understanding systems, mastering language, and positioning yourself like a player—not just a pawn.

And the rules? They weren't in schoolbooks. They were whispered in circles most of us never got invited to.

So I started studying. Quietly. Relentlessly.
Not just what rich people had, but how they moved.
How they thought. Where they put their money. What they prioritized. What they avoided. How they reacted when the market dropped. How they planted seeds and waited patiently, while the rest of us were chasing quick paychecks and tax returns.

And slowly, the patterns came into view. The playbook... the blueprint... became clear.

This book was born from that journey.
But it was also born from something else:
Frustration.

I got tired of people freezing up when I brought up stocks. Tired of the blank stares, the nervous laughs, the "I wish I knew more about that" responses. Even financial "professionals" would hesitate when the topic came up. Advisors who could sell you insurance, but couldn't break down an ETF. People treat the stock market like it's some mystical force—like magic only accessible to wizards in suits.

It's not magic.
It's not complicated (unless you want it to be).
And anyone can do it.

I wrote this book because I care.

Because I'm annoyed.

Because too many of us are out here hustling but staying broke.

Because the knowledge is out there—but no one's translating it.

Because too many people feel shame for not knowing what they were never taught.

I wrote it for the moment when your homie says, "I'm tryna get into stocks" but doesn't know where to start.

I wrote it for the cousin who works two jobs and still can't get ahead.

I wrote it for the kid on the block who's smarter than everyone in his school but doesn't know how to build wealth.

It wasn't written for trust fund babies.

It wasn't written for Wall Street analysts.

It was written for you.

For the reader who knows they were meant for more.

For the hustler who's tired of chasing the bag and ready to build something real.

For the first in their family to break the silence around money—and make wealth a normal conversation.

This ain't a textbook.

It's a translation.

It's the game in OUR language.

Plain. Sharp. Unapologetic.

Because I believe wealth should be teachable. Ownership should be common. And our people deserve more than just survival stories.

So if you're here to break generational curses, flip the script, and take control of your financial destiny? Then let's get to work. Let's flip the script. Let's rewrite the play. Let's build what they never thought we would.

So, in short, to answer your question bro, *"Yes"*. Yes, I f*ck with stocks. I buy them, sell them, trade them, profit off of them, and weaponize them.

And hopefully by the end, you will too.

— Niklaus Nasir

# ABOUT THE AUTHOR

The author didn't come from money. He came from motion and hustle. From ducking danger, clocking hours, and learning on the fly. From moving through a world that taught survival before it ever taught strategy. And yet, even then, he dreamed of sovereignty—not just making it out, but owning his future completely.

He was raised in a place where wealth was whispered about, but never shown. A place where people knew of money, but not its movements. Where the game was being played all around them, but no one was passing out rulebooks. Instead of accepting that silence, he chose to decode it. He studied the language of leverage. The psychology of power. The architecture of generational wealth. Not out of envy, but out of obsession.

He became a student of the game—not in some Ivy League classroom, but in the trenches. A product of both pain and potential, built from bounced checks and big ideas. He didn't just learn to chase the bag—he learned to understand the system behind the bag. The forces, incentives, loopholes, and levers that shape wealth in the real world.

From bouncing between jobs to launching side hustles. From working night shifts in security uniforms to cracking markets and decoding stock tickers. From watching others win to becoming the man in motion. He built his empire one insight at a time, one failure at a time, one win at a time. Not with a map, but with momentum.

He didn't wait for permission. He found the books. He cracked the codes. He listened when no one was talking and learned from the silence. He watched capital move, over and over again, until he could see the game before it happened.

Now, he writes not as some guru in a high tower, but as a translator. A codebreaker. A brother. A tactician with muddy boots and blood on his knuckles. Not to flex, but to equip. His words are aimed at the underdogs. The overlooked. The smart kids with no mentors. The wolves in sheep clothing, waiting to awaken.

If you've ever felt the hunger to rise but didn't know where to place your feet—this is for you. If you knew you were destined for more but couldn't find the blueprint—this is your signal.

His mission isn't just financial literacy—it's economic warfare. This is rebellion by education. Because the revolution the system fears most isn't loud—it's literate. It's strategic. It's well-read and well-armed with knowledge.

And trust—he's just getting started.

# TABLE OF CONTENTS

# INTRODUCTION
# YOU ALREADY INVEST EVERY DAY

L et's kill the noise upfront: you already invest. Chances are, you're just doing it wrong.

Every dollar you spend, every hour you burn on a screen, every move you make—it's all an investment: time, energy, money, attention. The question isn't *"Do you invest?"* The question is: *"Do you get a return?"*

Most people think investing is one of two things. First, some advanced, Ivy League, hedge-fund math thing. Or second, going all in on the latest crypto or penny stock, hoping it moons. Nah, bro. The truth is much deeper than that. Investing isn't complicated—and it isn't trendy. **Investing is ancient**.

Long before apps and stock tickers, people were already buying into systems they didn't have to touch. In ancient Mesopotamia, merchants carved agreements into clay tablets—grain loans, debt arrangements, early contracts. You could front somebody some seeds, and months later, get your cut back with interest. **That's investing.**

In the 1600s, the Dutch started selling shares in ships that hadn't even left the harbor. If the ship came back full? Everybody who bought in got paid. If it sank? You ate the loss. Risk and return, distributed among owners.

Then came the British East India Company. The Atlantic slave trade. The cotton empire. **Investments in brutality.** Profits pulled from blood.

And in America? The stock market grew on the backs of enslaved labor, war bonds, railroads, oil fields—all funded by people who never lifted a tool but got paid when others did.

That's the thread: **Ownership, not labor. Leverage, not sweat.** Wealth has always been about owning the system—not working inside it.

And while we don't need to repeat the methods that built the old empires—we *do* need to understand how they were built.
Our legacy doesn't have to be rooted in exploitation. But it does have to be rooted in **strategy**. Entrepreneurship. Equity. Execution.
**That's our lane now.**
We don't need blood to build. We need clarity, capital, and the courage to move different.

So let's dive in.

Today, when people hear "investing," a lot of them picture stockbrokers yelling or crypto bros flexing Lambos they probably leased. They think it's gambling. Or something only rich people do. Or that you need a finance degree just to get started.

Here's what it actually is: **Investing is the act of putting something in *now* to get something greater *later*.** That's it.

So when people say, *"I don't invest,"* what they're really saying is, *"I haven't figured out how to play the game they've been running since before my great-great-grandfather was born."*

**And that's why this book exists.**
To separate fact from fiction. To clear out the noise, the myths, the confusion. To equip you with the language, vision, and tools that actually work. To level the playing field. To give you the advantage.

To help you stop mistaking *movement* for *progress.*
To help you understand that investing isn't just about picking stocks—it's about choosing **yourself.**
It's about making decisions today that echo into a better tomorrow.
Not a get-rich scheme. Not a guessing game. A **system.** A **shift.**

You've been making moves all your life.
But were they stacking? Were they compounding? Were they putting you in position to win while you sleep?

This book is about alignment, precision, and ownership.
Not just surviving paycheck to paycheck—but creating flows that outlive your labor.
Not just reacting to money—but repositioning your life so money responds to **you.**

Because this world isn't waiting for you to catch up.
The game's been running—quietly and relentlessly. Every day you don't know the rules is a day you're being played. As P.T. Barnum famously said, "A sucker is born every minute." Lucky for you, this book will help you become sucker-free.

Lastly, understand this isn't a class. It's not a lecture. It's a conversation between me and you.

And we're gonna walk through:

- What investing actually is

- How to start with $10

- How to move from consumer to owner

- Why NOT investing is its own investment (albeit a poor one)

- Why long-term wealth is built, not found

- And how we can break the generational chains of poverty

Just because we're late to the game, doesn't make us locked out of the room.

This book opens the door. Step in. It's already yours.

CHAPTER 1

# NOBODY SHOWED US: WHY YOU WERE KEPT IN THE DARK

L et's get something straight: if nobody taught you how to invest, it's not because you weren't smart enough, bro. It's because they didn't know how to either.

They didn't teach it in school—not in real terms, and definitely not in ways that made sense to us. They taught us how to memorize dates and write essays, not how to build wealth, navigate markets, or flip the same tools the wealthy have been using for centuries.

And that's not an accident. The system benefits from your ignorance. If you don't know how money works, you'll spend it wrong. If you don't know how ownership works, you'll never demand a stake. If you don't know what wealth really is, you'll waste your life chasing the illusion of it.

This economy runs on your labor, your spending, and your silence. If you stay broke, distracted, and dependent—it stays fed.

Your parents? Your people? Most of them were in survival mode. You don't talk about index funds when the lights might get cut off. You don't plan a 401(k) when the fridge is empty. They passed down hustle, not strategy. Work ethic, not equity.

But let's be real—they weren't lazy. They weren't dumb. They were just playing defense in a game where the scoreboard was hidden. They gave you what they had: rules for getting by, not rules for getting ahead.

You might've been told:

- "Go to school. Get a good job."
- "Save your money."
- "Stay outta debt."

And that's not bad advice. It's just incomplete.

Because what they didn't say was:

- How to **grow** your money.
- How to **protect** your money.
- How to **own something** that earns while you sleep.

They taught you to earn—not to invest. They taught you how to grind—not how to multiply. And that's why most people stay stuck. Chasing money that never stays long. Trading time for checks, then spending those checks on things that don't return anything but a moment of comfort. Nobody told us that comfort costs—and that investing is just delayed comfort, but *forever*.

The deeper truth? The old blueprint doesn't work anymore. That whole "work 30 years, retire with a pension" model? That was the script for another generation. In this AI-powered, data-driven, constantly shifting economy, jobs are getting automated. Roles are being outsourced. People are becoming replaceable. Even trading is being done by bots.

But don't get it twisted—while bots are powerful tools, they still need to be trained, maintained, and updated. And a bot can't set the vision for your life. Only you can do that. And if you're reading this book, you've already proven one thing: you're ambitious.

In this economy, the people who win will be the ones who adapt. Who learn high-demand skills. Who automate. Who multiply their time. This book is part of that journey. It's not just about investing in stocks—it's about investing in yourself. So if this is your first time hearing this? Good. That means this is your moment. The break in the cycle. The starting point.

This chapter is here to help you:

- Rewire how you see money
- Understand why you were never given the blueprint
- Realize that just because you were behind doesn't mean you stay there

No shame, only game.

Let's start with the most important truth from here on out, bro:

**You're not stupid. You're just first-generation wealth-aware.**

Now let's get into what they never taught you—and what you're about to learn for yourself.

*"You've been hoodwinked, bamboozled, run amuck, and led astray!" - Malcolm X*

*"It is easier to fool someone, than convince someone they have been fooled" - Mark Twain*

*"In the land of the blind, the one-eyed man is king" - Desiderius Erasmus*

# CHAPTER 2

# THE GAME AIN'T NEW: INVESTING IS ANCIENT

You might think all this investing stuff is modern—apps, charts, crypto, CNBC—but don't let the tech fool you. Investing is ancient.

Let's break it down.

Long before Wall Street, people were building wealth by putting up capital, taking risks, and owning pieces of something bigger than themselves. The tools have changed. The plays have evolved. But the concept? It's been around since humans figured out how to trade. The barter system was investing. Lending grain was investing. Holding gold? That was saving and flexing at the same time. Property was power. And yes—slavery was an investment too. The transatlantic slave trade, while brutal and dehumanizing, was a billion-dollar industry. The ownership of people, of labor, of output—that's how the "New World," the Americas, were built: on portfolios of human suffering.

Understand this: **Wealth has never been random. It's always been engineered.**

In ancient Mesopotamia, people lent out grain, recorded debts on clay tablets, and collected returns with interest. In ancient Africa, marketplaces weren't just about trade—they were full-blown financial ecosystems. Gold, salt, ivory, textiles—commerce was flowing long before a single stock ticker ever existed. In China, silk was more than fashion—it was economic power. The Silk Road wasn't just a trade route; it was an international wealth pipeline. Dynasties were built off of thread. Arab traders moved incense, precious metals, mathematics, astronomy—and yes, early forms of chemical engineering that would later evolve into what the West called "gunpowder." That was commerce at scale.

Then came the Dutch and the first stock exchanges. The British East India Company. Colonial empires built off shares, profits, and structured ownership. You weren't rich because you worked hard. You were rich because you owned—the boats, the banks, the land, the people. As time went on, the systems evolved, but the game stayed the same. Banks emerged to protect the wealth of those who already had it. Insurance companies insured slave ships. Governments handed out land grants and oil rights—but only to people in the right rooms. The playing field was never fair.

And even now? The real bag is still hidden behind the curtain: trust funds, shell companies, tax loopholes, real estate trusts, business acquisitions, IPO allocations. People who don't look like you have been playing this game on God mode for centuries. And they pass it down, generation after generation, like an heirloom—while the rest of us sit on the sidelines wondering what we missed.

So what does any of this even mean? How does it help *you*?

Well, bro, we start with what we have. Today, nearly all of us have access to a smartphone or computer. With those tools, we can invest in publicly traded companies ourselves—ideally, companies we already use and understand. Why, though? Because when you buy a share of Apple, or any other company, you're not just "buying a stock." You're stepping into a legacy. A centuries-old structure where ownership, not labor, is the real source of wealth. You're not just investing in phones—you're buying into infrastructure, systems, and influence. Same moves the Dutch made in 1602—just digitized, streamlined, and globalized.

Once you understand that, you realize something powerful: the system was never designed to pay you. It was designed to use you—unless you flip your position. From consumer to owner. From employee to investor. From subject to sovereign.

We were taught to be labor. To be loyal. To consume. But wealth has always flowed toward ownership.
You've always been in the game—you just didn't know where your seat was.
This isn't about reinventing the wheel. It's about finally owning it.

We're not new to the grind—we're new to the paperwork.
We're not new to value—we're new to the valuation.

Because peep this: history used to belong to the wealthy. If you weren't born into it or schooled into it, you didn't get the playbook. Knowledge was locked behind walls—libraries, universities, private clubs. But now? The entire system is wide open. We live in the most connected, digitized, information-rich era in human history. Everything you want to learn—investing, trading, real estate, AI, automation—is available at the tap of a screen, the click of a button, or a voice command.

You are no longer excluded because of your family name, your skin color, your bank account, your accent, or your God.

*The only things that separate you from the wealth you seek are skill, acumen, and personal ambition.*

This book—and this series—will help you build the skill. It'll also give you the acumen as well. But as for the ambition? That's on you. That's your job.

And it's okay to be afraid. That just means it matters. That means you've got skin in the game. But don't ever let fear be your excuse. Because as the saying goes - *scared money don't make no money.*

Statistically speaking - you've only got 28,854 days on this planet, give or take a few. About a third of that time is spent before you can legally buy a drink. (21 if you're in the United States)

So - time is not unlimited, bro. It's of the essence. And if you're reading this, you've already outlived some people who never got the chance to read a page like this.

You're late to the game—but you're still in it. And if you play it right? You might just rewrite the rules.

> *"Better late than never, but never late is better." - Aubrey 'Drake' Graham*

> *"The best time to plant a tree was 20 years ago. The second-best time is now." - Chinese Proverb*

> *"Start late. Start over. Start scared. Just start." - Mel Robbins*

# CHAPTER 3

# WHAT EVEN IS A STOCK?: THE KEYS OF OWNERSHIP

L et's break it all the way down.

You hear people talk about buying stocks, owning shares, flipping options, going short, going long—blah blah blah. But nobody ever stops to explain what the hell a *stock* actually is. And because nobody explains it clearly, most folks stay confused, stay intimidated, or worse—stay out the game entirely.

So let's fix that.

In its simplest form, **a stock is a piece of ownership in a company**. That's it. When you buy stock, you're not just throwing money at a brand you like. You're literally buying a fraction of the business structure itself. *Point blank, period*. If that business grows? You eat. If it crashes? You feel that too. But the key is—you're not a customer anymore. You're an owner.

Let's say a company has one million shares, and you own 100 of them—or 10, or 1, or even just a fraction of one. It doesn't matter how small the slice is—ownership is ownership. That's your cut. That's your seat at the table. And just like with any table, you don't need to own the whole meal to eat—you just need a plate. When they win, you win.

# Where Do Stocks Come From, Bro?

Good question.

Stocks are created when a private company decides to go public—usually through something called an **IPO**, or **Initial Public Offering**. It's a major move. During an IPO, a company basically slices itself into pieces (shares) and offers those pieces to the public in exchange for capital (money). That capital is then used to grow the business—maybe to expand operations, launch a new product line, pay off debt, or scale into new markets.

Going public means stepping onto a bigger stage. With that comes regulation, SEC filings, financial transparency, and accountability to shareholders. In exchange? Access to massive amounts of money and the ability to grow at scale.

Once public, the company's stock becomes available on exchanges like the NYSE or Nasdaq, and anyone with a brokerage app—Robinhood, Cash App, Fidelity, etc.—can grab shares.

Now, not every company goes public. Some choose to stay private—keeping ownership tight between founders, early investors, and insiders. Getting in on a private company is rare and usually reserved for venture capitalists or high-net-worth players. High risk, high reward.

But going public? That's when the game opens up. That's why IPOs are a big deal. The company sets an initial number of shares and a starting price. But after that? The market decides what it's worth. Supply, demand, news, earnings, hype—it all gets baked into the stock price in real time.

# Different Types of Shares

Not all shares are created equal. Some companies issue multiple classes of stock—like Class A, Class B, and Class C.

Without going too deep, here's the basic gist:

- **Class A** shares usually come with more voting rights or special perks for early investors or founders.

- **Class B** shares might have reduced voting power but are often more widely available to the public.

- **Class C** shares typically have no voting rights but still let you ride the wave if the company grows.

Now beyond classes, there's also a difference between common and preferred stock.

**Common stock** is what most retail investors (you and I) will be buying through apps like Robinhood or Fidelity. It gives you ownership in the company and potential dividends—but the real value is in the price going up over time.

**Preferred stock**, on the other hand, usually pays a fixed dividend and gets paid out before common stockholders if the company ever goes under. It's kind of a blend between a stock and a bond. Less risky, but usually with less upside.

For most people, common stock is the move—and it's what you'll be holding in most brokerage accounts.

Ownership is still ownership. And your money still works for you.

Some common stocks pay dividends, which is basically the company cutting you in on a percentage of the profits—profits meaning what's left after expenses get paid (revenue minus costs = profit). Like,

"Thanks for riding with us—here's your slice." It's passive income. You didn't clock in. You just held the asset.

Other stocks don't pay dividends but grow in value over time, meaning you can sell your shares later for more than you bought them. That's called **capital gains**. Think of it like buying a rare collectible—let's say a limited-edition sneaker. You cop it for $200. Years later, people are willing to pay $800 because there's fewer of them out there and demand is up. Same idea. Scarcity and demand push price. But here's the key: scarcity alone doesn't guarantee a price spike. It's the demand for that scarce asset—or more specifically, the *perceived value* of it—that really moves the needle.

Stocks aren't limited like sneakers, but when a company's future looks bright, people rush in. That demand drives price up. It's not about rarity—it's about relevance.

So why does this matter? Because when you start thinking like an owner, your entire relationship with money changes. You stop chasing clout and start chasing compound interest. You stop blowing cash on things that look good today but hold no value tomorrow. Instead, you start planting your money in vehicles that grow quietly while you sleep. Ownership puts you in a position where your money works harder than you do.

You stop wasting money on stuff that fades and start planting seeds in systems that scale.

Nike sells you shoes. But Nike stock pays you back. Apple sells you a phone. But Apple stock gets you paid when they sell more.
You can wear the brand—or you can own it.

This chapter is about flipping that mindset. Understanding the power of ownership. And learning how to spot the difference between *looking* rich and *getting* rich.

> *"If you can't explain it to a six-year-old, you don't understand it yourself." - Albert Einstein*

> *"Now is the time to get knowledge, or end in a pit of ignorance" - Wallace Fard Muhammad*

> *"The greatest enemy of knowledge is not ignorance, it is the illusion of knowledge." - Stephen Hawking*

## CHAPTER 4

# LONG GAME VS. FAST MONEY: THE DIFFERENCE BETWEEN INVESTING & TRADING

Let's be real—everybody wants to get paid. Some want it slow and steady, others want it fast and loud.

But before we go any further, let's make sure we know what we're talking about.

**Investing** is the *long game*. You're buying pieces of strong companies, holding them for years, and letting your money grow quietly in the background. You're not trying to double your money in a day—you're playing the compound interest game, building wealth brick by brick.

**Trading** is the *fast lane*. You're jumping in and out of positions—stocks, options, crypto, whatever's moving—with the goal of making profit in the short term. It's more intense. More hands-on. More risk. But when done right? It can move your bag quickly.

Two different approaches. Same mission: get to the money.

Let's dive in.

# The Long Game = Wealth (The Quiet Stack)

Long-term investing is slow, patient, and powerful. It's what builds wealth quietly over time. Think retirement accounts. Think compound interest. Think holding great companies for years and letting them grow. The moves are small, but the timeline is long—and the gains? They stack.

When you invest for the long game, you're not chasing hype. You're betting on **consistency**. You're letting your money marinate. You're building a foundation that frees you from check-to-check living.

This is your 401(k), your Roth IRA, your index funds. This is where you buy, hold, and chill.

You're not looking for quick flips—you're focused on long-term growth. That means putting your money into companies or funds you believe in and letting time do what it does best. You're not chasing a bag every day—you're building one that grows slowly, steadily, and securely.

Examples:

- Contributing monthly to an S&P 500 index fund
- Setting aside a portion of your weekly or monthly income to buy shares of companies like Apple, Microsoft, or Costco for 5–10+ years
- Reinvesting your dividends so your money compounds over time

This is where consistency beats intensity. You build the habit. You feed the machine. And over time, the machine feeds you.

Personally? This is the **core** of how I invest. I look at the world I live in and ask: *What companies are going to grow—and what companies are going to die?*

I'll joke with friends sometimes:

"Yo, I got a business idea. It's a video rental store. You walk in, grab a VHS tape, then bring it back in three days. I'm calling it Blockbuster. You in?"

Obviously, they say no—because that business model is done.

Same thing when I ask, "Would you invest in a brand-new coal company right now?" Again, no. Because the world is moving toward electric, solar, wind, and other renewable energy sources.

Ultimately, this is what long-term investing is really about: **pattern recognition**. Seeing where the world is headed and putting your money on the future—not the past. You're not just buying stock. **You're buying where the world is going.**

## FOUNDATION CHECK:

That one line—"You're buying where the world is going"—is the cornerstone. It's the entire philosophy of this book, this series, this mindset.

If that lands for you?
Mission accomplished. You get it. You *are* it. You don't need another chart, another stat, or another chapter. You've already uncovered the secret.

Everything after this is just refinement. Enhancement. Bonus game. Stick around if you want the layers—but if you left right here, you'd still be good. You're holding the key.
The only question now is: *how far do you want to go?*

Let's continue.

## The Fast Lane = Cash Flow (The Skill Play)

This is the fast lane. This is where you catch short-term price moves, flip positions, and turn volatility into opportunity. You're not just holding for years—you're moving with intention. Trading in this lane might mean swing trading, day trading, scalping, flipping options contracts, trading futures, or running structured multi-leg strategies like iron condors, straddles, or credit spreads.

But here's the thing: **fast money isn't just "hoping it goes up."** Advanced trading gives you the tools to profit in any scenario— whether prices rise, fall, or stay neutral. Directional plays let you bet on movement. Neutral strategies pay when the market stays in range. The key isn't guessing—it's precision.

You get that precision from structure. You craft strategies using a mix of technical indicators, fundamental analysis, market sentiment, and your personal risk tolerance. It's not emotional. It's calculated. **It's arithmetic**.

You're not investing—you're extracting. You're in the market to make moves, not sit and wait.

This is active income. You're not just watching candles on a chart— you're reading behavior. Volume, momentum, support and resistance, trend shifts, and news catalysts all shape the battlefield. You set your entries, exits, and stop-losses like a tactician. You move fast—but never without a plan.

It gets deep—and yes, we'll dive into all of that in *Aye Bro, You Tryna Trade Forreal?* (the second book in this series). But understand this: active trading is warfare. And before you fight that war, you need field training.

Just like you can't claim a set without putting in the work, you can't just "hop in" the market without earning your stripes. As a wise man once said:

*"Don't let your mouth overload your ass."*

In trading? Don't let your ego overload your bankroll.

Learn the basics. Train the reps. Study the field. Or the market will humble you—fast.

Don't be fooled by highlight reels and flex posts. Just because someone shows a $10,000 win doesn't mean they're actually profitable. You didn't see the losses. You didn't see the sleepless nights. The over-leveraged plays. The blown-up accounts.

When it works, it works fast. But when it fails? It fails hard. Belts are put to bottoms.
Asses—spanked.

That's why it's called a *skill play*. Not gambling. Execution. It demands discipline, emotional control, and relentless study.

Personally? I treat trading like a martial art. You don't freestyle karate. You train. You practice. You build a system that fits you—your life, your risk, your rhythm.

You're not just chasing a quick bag.
You're learning how to read money in motion.

## So Which One is Best, Bro?

Some people act like you have to pick sides—either you're Warren Buffett, holding blue chips for decades, or you're a hoodie-wearing day trader glued to ten monitors. But the smart ones? They don't choose. They adapt. They zoom out, learn the rules of both games, and use them strategically—long game for wealth, fast game for cash flow—knowing exactly when to lean in and when to pull back.

Because here's the truth: markets move in cycles. Bull runs, bear markets, sideways chop—each one requires a different approach. In some seasons, it's smarter to play defense and sit on your long-term positions. In others, opportunity is flying across your screen every hour, and the traders are eating. The pros don't "pick one." They master both. They're flexible. Fluid. Surgical.

Use fast money to build your bankroll. Use long-term investing to build your freedom. Use trading to get liquid. Use investing to get leverage. You eat today with short-term flips. You escape the rat race with long-term stacks.

Learn both. Then learn yourself. What's your temperament? Your schedule? Your risk tolerance? Your end goal? It's not about copying someone else's blueprint—it's about designing your own. This isn't a one-size-fits-all path. It's a toolkit. And depending on your goals, your season, and your risk appetite, you'll reach for different tools at different times.

This chapter wasn't just about stocks or setups. It was about mindset. About options. Control. Awareness. So you can stop guessing, stop choosing between now and later—and finally start stacking both with purpose.

> *"I never attempt to make money on the stock market. I buy on the assumption that they could close the market the next day and not reopen it for five years." - Warren Buffett*

> *"In trading, It's not whether you're right or wrong that's important, but how much money you make when you're right and how much you lose when you're wrong." - George Soros*

> *"Compound interest is the eighth wonder of the world. He who understands it, earns it... he who doesn't, pays it." - Albert Einstein*

# CHAPTER 5

# START WHERE YOU ARE: HOW TO BEGIN WITH ONLY TEN DOLLARS

So by now you're sold on the vision. You understand the difference between long game and fast money. You're ready to stop being a consumer and start being an owner.

But then reality hits: you look at your bank account and wonder if you've got enough to even play.

Good news? **You don't need thousands to start.** You don't even need hundreds. You can get in this game with ten dollars.

No cap, no bap.

Because this chapter isn't about having money—it's about building momentum.

## The $10 Shift

Let's get one thing clear: starting small isn't embarrassing—it's strategic. It's like going to the gym for the first time and picking up the 10-pound dumbbells. You're not trying to show off—you're building form.

Same with investing. You start with what you have. Then you build consistency. Then you build strength.

Apps like Cash App, Robinhood, Public, or Fidelity let you buy fractional shares. That means you don't need to buy a full share of Apple or Tesla—you can buy $10 worth. You're still an owner. Still in the game.

Set a goal: $10 a week. That's $40 a month. $480 a year. Add in compound growth over time—and now we're talking.

## I Don't Have $10, Bro...

Then, brother—you've got a deeper challenge on your hands. And that's neither a shade or a diss. But it's facts.

If you don't have $10 a week, you either have;
**1.)** a spending problem, or
**2.)** an income problem.

And either one? Can be fixed.

This book isn't therapy. But here's a little real talk:

### 1. Spending Problem: Spending Above Your Means

**Stop.** Right now. Your power lies in your ability to simplify. Frugality isn't weakness—it's control.

You don't need to give up everything. But you do need to start seeing things through a new lens: **assets vs. liabilities**. If it drains your wallet and doesn't build your future? **Cut it**.

That might mean it's time to stop buying fast food every day. Maybe it's time to meal prep. Maybe cancel one of those five streaming services you barely use. The goal isn't punishment—it's positioning.

Far too many people try to look rich on social media while their real bank account says otherwise—if they even have one. They buy the latest fashion and tech just to "keep up with the Joneses." You see them online and think, *"Damn, I wish I lived like them..."* Brother, it's a lie. You don't see the past-due notices. You don't see the endless *"Can you send me a Cash App?"* texts. You don't see any of it. Most of these folks are robbing Peter to pay Paul, and their debt is as high as their follower count.

So if this is you, bro... stop. Stop trying to impress people who don't care about you. Stop chasing dopamine and followers. It's okay to take a momentary step back in order to set up a grand leap forward. If you've got to eat ramen for a while, you'll be alright. If you're rocking the same old iPhone, that's fine. If you've got to keep the hoopty instead of getting the Hellcat? It's. Okay.

Delayed doesn't mean denied. You can have everything you want—one day. But you've got to build the foundation first. Because if you keep fucking off your money, you'll always be chasing it. You'll never be free.

And what good is life without freedom?

As Tyler Durden famously said, *"The things you own, end up owning you."*

## 2. Income Problem: You're Broke

You need to take inventory, bro.

Let me tell you something real. When I was just starting out, I didn't have an in-demand skill either. I bounced from minimum wage job to minimum wage job, hoping I'd pick up extra hours so I could make more money. But no matter how much I worked, I never made any real progress with my earnings—until I realized something:

Why is it that a fast food worker is paid >$15/hour to flip burgers, while a surgeon easily makes $100/hour or more?

The answer is simple: **the *value* of the skill itself**.
Virtually anyone can flip a burger or mop a floor. (Honestly, a monkey could be trained to do it—sanitation standards aside.) But there are only around 34,000 ABS-certified surgeons in the U.S. as of 2025. How much harder is it to perform surgery than flip a burger? I'll let you answer that one.

Now don't miss the forest for the trees—I'm not saying you need to go to medical school to level up. Not even close. But if you're income-challenged (you're broke), you must gain a skill. That could be website building, SEO, marketing, barbering, landscaping, sales—you name it. The sky's the limit. You just need to choose a path.

For me, I chose security. I watched my grandfather—no college degree, just a high school diploma—work for CPS (Chicago Public Schools) for over 30 years. He bought a home and retired with dignity—all off of that security money. That kind of legacy stuck with me.

I was a product of both love and abuse. Someone who attended both public and private schools. I saw wealth close enough to smell it, but never taste it. I felt poverty deeply, but never became a subject of it. I also grew up fighting. Violence wasn't just familiar—it felt like the only thing I was ever naturally good at. It gave me control. Power. And eventually—a path.

I learned how to turn that into something real.
I realized a commanding presence and aggressive disposition could be a skill, just as powerful as any degree. Security certifications were cheap—less than $500 total. I became a legally hired gun. Paid for my presence. My toughness. My ability to control space. For once, the thing that made me feel dangerous also made me feel useful.

And again—don't miss the forest for the trees. I'm not saying you should become a security guard.

What I *am* saying is this: **there's demand for damn near anything**.

Start by taking inventory of who you are. What you've survived. What you naturally gravitate toward. What you do better than most. Whatever that is—there's a market for it. You just need to identify it. Sharpen it. Sell it.

You need only to **INVEST**. That's the thread. That's the whole play. Whether it's stocks, skills, or self—it's all the same muscle. Build it. Back it. Bet on it.

So let me ask you:
Do you have a skill that's in demand? If so, how are you using your time? Are you charging enough? Are you building toward something?

And if you don't have a valuable skill—don't panic. Start learning one. Choose something aligned with your goals, your temperament, your personality. Something that fits how you want to live.

Ask yourself: *What am I willing to exchange for the wealth I seek?*
**Because all wealth is a trade**—time for money, skill for opportunity, energy for execution.

No one's coming to save you. But you can save yourself.
Start where you are. Even if it's $10 and a mindset shift—that's still movement.
That's still ownership.
And that's how this game begins.

## What Do I Buy First, Bro?

When you're starting with a small bankroll, your best bet is **index funds** or **ETFs**. These are collections of stocks—think of them like a sampler platter of the market. Instead of betting everything on one company, you're spreading your risk across hundreds.

ETFs can be divided by sector, industry, market cap, geographic region, volatility, and more. Whether you want to focus on energy, tech, healthcare, emerging markets, or even dividend-paying giants—there's an ETF for that.

Look into:

- VOO or SPY – S&P 500
- VTI – Total U.S. market
- QQQ – Tech-focused index
- IEMG or EEM – Emerging markets
- XLV – Healthcare sector
- VNQ – Real estate (REITs)

These aren't fast-flip plays—although they can be used that way as part of a strategy (see: Aye Bro, You Be Trading Forreal)—they're largely stable, steady, and proven. They grow as the economy grows. And here's the beautiful part—because your capital is still small, even big market downturns can work in your favor. When prices dip, it means you're buying the same assets on sale. As long as you stay consistent and keep contributing, you're stacking more shares for less.

## The Real Winner? Behavior

Starting with $10 builds a habit. A routine. It reprograms your brain from **spender** to **investor**.
You stop asking, *"What can I buy today?"* and start asking, *"What can I build today?"*

Because in this game, **consistency crushes size**. Ten dollars a week might not change your life this month—but over five years? That's how portfolios are born.

And here's the bonus: **investing can double as a smarter form of saving**.
Think about it—saving means putting money aside that you don't need to touch right now. So why let it sit somewhere doing nothing? You can park that same money in a stable ETF, and not only are you saving, you're building. You're giving your savings a job.

Most savings accounts pay close to zero interest. Even the better ones—like high-yield savings accounts (HYSAs) or Treasury accounts—might give you 4–5% a year. That's cute. But smart investing, over the long term? It's historically returned **7–10% annually**, depending on your portfolio. And unlike a savings account, it scales fast when you stay consistent.

This isn't about gambling your rent money. It's about using money you don't need right now and setting it up to **grow**. As your income increases, your savings rate—and your **investment** rate—should increase too.

**Set it and forget it.**
Almost every app mentioned—Cash App, Fidelity, Robinhood, Public—lets you automate deposits. Even $10 or $25 a week, automatically pulled from your checking account and dropped into an ETF, starts stacking **without you even thinking about it**. Invisible wealth.

That's called **dollar-cost averaging**—buying a little at a time, regardless of what the market is doing. It smooths out volatility, builds discipline, and protects you from overthinking.

You don't need a bag to start.
**You need a habit.**

So whether you've got $10, $100, or $1,000—the blueprint stays the same:

- Pick your platform.
- Pick your ETF.
- Set your amount.
- Automate the deposit.
- Let it run.

You don't need to watch it every day. Just build the system—and let the system build your future.

> *"The secret of getting ahead is getting started."* - Mark Twain

> *"The journey of a thousand miles begins with a single step."* - Lao Tzu

> *"If I had six hours to chop down a tree, I'd spend the first four sharpening the axe."* - Abraham Lincoln

# CHAPTER 6

# FROM CONSUMER TO OWNER: A SHIFT IN MINDSET

By this point, you've started to see the game differently. You know you can start small. You know how to buy into the market. But this next shift? **It's not about the money—it's about identity**.

The truth is, most people stay broke not because they lack potential, but because they never shift out of the **consumer mindset**. We've been conditioned to think like spenders. We wear our worth. We finance our status. We chase dopamine in the form of Instagram likes, follower counts, and impulse buys—instead of dividends. We celebrate liabilities and ignore assets. Worse—we *mistake* the former for the latter. And the system loves it that way.

We earn just to spend. We hustle just to flex. We work our whole lives to buy things that make us *feel* rich—but never actually **make us rich**.

But not you. **You're moving different.** You're learning the game piece by piece—and becoming dangerous.

This chapter is about **flipping your role** in the system. It's about becoming the type of person who doesn't just make purchases but makes plays—*real* plays.

Because ownership isn't just about having money—it's about having position. It's a shift in how you see yourself. Not as a customer. Not as a follower. But as a **shareholder**. A **builder**. A **boss**.

You've been on the wrong side of the equation for too long. **It's time to cross over.**

## Ownership Is a Mindset

Owning a stock isn't just about percentages—it's about position. When you become a shareholder, even with just $10, you've taken a step outside of the consumer class. You're no longer just feeding the machine—you own part of it. Every dollar you invest is a vote for what you believe will grow. A claim on future value. A slice of power. And when you get intentional about where you place those dollars, you stop feeling powerless in this system. You start realizing the same tools that built dynasties are now in your hands.

This isn't about being rich today—it's about learning how rich people *think*, and how they *move*. They're not focused on being liked. They're focused on leverage. They don't chase every trend. They plant seeds in systems they understand. And trends? They're everywhere, especially in the financial world. Every hour there's a new crypto coin, penny stock, and a Reddit thread screaming *"it's going to the moon!"* (It's not.)

Don't get swept up in the noise. Don't invest in things you don't understand. If you can't explain what it is, what it does, and why you believe in it—**stay away**. At that point, you're not investing or trading. You're gambling. Worse—you're just pissing in the wind. If your dollars are your soldiers and you're the general, buying things you don't understand is like marching your troops straight into an ambush. Don't do it.

This is about a mindset shift—from trying to look rich to becoming rich. From chasing clout to compounding. From being impressed by power to possessing it. Ownership is the difference. And once you taste it, you'll never go back.

## Start Seeing Everything Through Equity

Look around you. Every product you use, every brand you rep, every monthly charge on your bank statement—it's all part of someone else's empire. Your favorite phone brand? Public company. That streaming service you binge on weekends? Public. The fast food franchise? Public. Even the sneakers on your feet? Stock ticker attached.

So let's ask the real question: Why *just* consume, when you can also *own*? If you spend money with them, why not make money with them? Every time you tap your card, you're swiping into someone else's revenue stream. You're feeding their ecosystem, their stock price, their board's bonuses, their generational wealth.

Flip the script. **Start treating your purchases like data points**. Each swipe is a clue to where you're already positioned—just on the wrong side. You don't need to be a Wall Street analyst to build a watchlist. Just study your own habits.

**Start asking:**

*"Do I spend money here every month?"*

*"Is this part of my lifestyle or just a one-time hype buy?"*

*"Would I want a cut of this company's long-term growth?"*

*"If I had a chance to invest in this business before it blew up, would I have taken it?"*

Because newsflash—you do. Every single day. That's the twist most people miss. These aren't just stocks. These are the systems you're already helping to grow. If you're paying for Netflix every month, why not hold a slice of it? If you never go a day without your iPhone, why not let Apple pay you back?

**Ownership isn't about being perfect—it's about being aware.** And once you start seeing everything through the lens of equity, your whole worldview changes. You stop being impressed by brands. You start studying the business model. You stop throwing your money away. You start planting it in places that work for you.

Every swipe, every stream, every delivery, every device—it's either feeding someone else's future, or helping you build your own.

## Own What You Use

You already spend money. You already have habits. So instead of trying to change your whole lifestyle overnight—just align it with ownership.

If you wear Nike, own Nike ($NKE).
If you use an iPhone daily, own Apple ($AAPL).
If you shop at Target, own Target ($TGT).
If you can't stop scrolling Instagram—Meta owns that ($META). Own them back.

This isn't about guilt-tripping your spending. It's about turning your routine into a return. You don't have to stop consuming—you just have to start converting. When your purchases and your portfolio match up, your lifestyle becomes leverage. You start getting paid from both sides: the front-end (what you buy) and the back-end (what you own).

It's not just about being in the system—it's about tapping into it. Monetizing your own loyalty.

Own what you wear. Own what you eat. Own what you click.
Make your habits profitable.

## The Goal Is Ownership

As you already know, this book isn't just about fast flips. Fast flips are cool—but they're only one piece of the puzzle. What we're really after is financial fluency. The kind that lets you breathe different, move different. The kind that starts with ownership.

Envision every dollar you earn as a tool—and every tool you master brings you closer to freedom. Your dollars should be working just as hard as you do—if not harder. You have a limited amount of time and energy. But your money? That can compound forever. So put it to work.

Ownership is the difference between reacting to life and designing it. It's the bridge between survival and strategy. Between hoping and building. And that bridge starts the moment you decide:
*"I'm done watching other people eat. It's time I took a seat at the table."*

Because once you shift your mindset from earning to owning, everything else recalibrates:
Your priorities shift—from **spending to stacking**.
Your circle sharpens—from **distractions to alignment**.
Your goals stop being wishes—and **start becoming systems**.

This is more than a financial shift. It's a full-blown philosophical one. A different way of seeing yourself. Of seeing money. Of seeing the world. It's about reclaiming control—not just over your wallet, but over your destiny. It's about choosing power. Not just witnessing it. Not just begging for it. Not just wielding it.
But enacting it. Weaponizing it.

We're not asking for a seat.

We're positioning ourselves at the head of the table.

Because when you own something, you're no longer just living in the world—you're shaping it.

> *"We can't become what we need to be by remaining what we are."* — *Oprah Winfrey*

> *"Progress is impossible without change, and those who cannot change their minds cannot change anything."* — *George Bernard Shaw*

> *"The best way to see the future is to create it."* — *Peter Drucker*

# CHAPTER 7

# SCARED MONEY DON'T MAKE MONEY: WHY FEAR KEEPS YOU BROKE

Getting money is one thing. Keeping it? That's important. But growing it? That's where most people freeze.

Why? Because of fear.

This chapter is about deconstructing fear—fear of the market, fear of loss, fear of not knowing enough, and fear of stepping out of your comfort zone. Because here's the truth:

**Scared money doesn't just miss out—it doesn't learn.**

## Risk Is Real—But So Is Stagnation

As we've already come to understand by now... yeah, investing carries risk. Your money can dip. The market can wobble. Things can go left. Recessions hit. Portfolios turn red. Bad headlines drop. Companies miss earnings. These are all part of the game, bro.

But you know what else is risky? **Doing nothing**.

Inflation eats your savings. Opportunities pass you by. Compound growth skips you. And the clock doesn't stop ticking. Every year you sit out, your future purchasing power shrinks. Every year you delay is a year you pushed financial freedom further away.

So let's be clear: *not investing* **IS** *a risk*. It just feels safer because the losses are **invisible**.

But silence is expensive. Comfort costs. And inaction is still a choice.

## Sitting Out Is a Trade, Bro

Not putting your money in the market is a decision. It's a trade—just one with zero upside. You're trading uncertainty for stagnation. And in most cases? It's a losing one.

Because the market doesn't wait. It doesn't pause until you "feel ready." It rewards the consistent, not the perfect. You don't get bonus points for watching from the sidelines.

Think about it: while you're waiting to feel confident, somebody else with less education, less experience, and less capital is pressing 'buy'. They're not smarter than you—they're just in motion. They're letting time do what time does: stack.

Fear convinces you to sit still. But time punishes stillness.

## Don't Get Tricked Out of Your Position

The market, while inanimate—deaf, blind, heartless—moves. It goes through phases. Cycles. Just like the economy.

**Market Phases**:

- **Accumulation** – Smart money buys when prices are low and sentiment is quiet

- **Markup** – Prices begin rising, optimism returns, momentum builds

- **Distribution** – Prices peak, volume increases, smart money exits

- **Decline** – Panic selling, lower highs and lower lows, market cools off

**Economic Cycle:**

- **Expansion** – GDP grows, jobs rise, optimism returns

- **Peak** – Economy overheats, inflation creeps in

- **Contraction** – Growth slows, layoffs begin, fear enters

- **Trough** – The low point; time to rebuild and reset

While they may appear similar, the market and the economy are not the same. The market is forward-looking—it moves on expectations. By the time you *feel* the economy hurting, the market may already be rebounding. That's why it pays to stay disciplined. And stay in.

So when folks start yelling about the dollar going to zero or the whole system collapsing—**relax**. This book isn't propaganda, but facts are facts: the U.S. is still an economic juggernaut. Will there be volatility? Of course. Will it all burn down tomorrow? Both highly and widely unlikely.

More importantly, just because you live in the U.S. doesn't mean you're stuck with the U.S. market. The world is bigger than one country. Global opportunities exist. And to the international bros reading this— whether you're in Europe, Asia, Africa, or the Middle East—assets are global. Don't get sucked into someone's apocalyptic doomsday fantasy. Keep calm and carry on.

Bottom line? Downturns are for buying, not crying—especially if your time horizon is long and you're still in grind mode.

The only time downturns become a real threat is when you're nearing retirement and need to start living off your portfolio. If that's you, it's a different game. You move conservative, shift out of risk, and protect what you've built.

But for most reading this? You've got time. You've got energy. You've got the ability to ride the waves—and stack while others panic.

## Playing Safe ≠ Not Playing

This isn't about being reckless. It's about being active.

You don't need to YOLO your savings into a hot stock. You don't need to turn into a full-time trader. But you do need to put your money to work. You need to start learning the game while you're still close enough to the bottom to afford small losses. Start with ETFs. Start with fractional shares. Start with what you understand. Start with what you can afford to lose.

There's a difference between being cautious and being frozen.

Being cautious says: *"Let me study before I move."*

Being frozen says: *"I'm too scared to try."*

**Only <u>one</u> of those builds wealth.**

Because real investors aren't fearless. They're strategic. They take calculated risks. They stay in motion.

## The Biggest Risk Is Never Showing Up

You don't have to time the market. You don't need to know every chart pattern. You don't have to be the smartest person in the room. You just have to show up. Be willing to try. Willing to fail forward. Willing to learn, pivot, and refine your process.

Because scared money doesn't just miss shots—it never gets in the gym. And nobody builds muscle from the parking lot.

You can read books. Watch YouTube. Scroll Twitter. But at some point, you've got to take a swing. You've got to place a trade. You've got to risk a little to learn a lot.

Here's the truth: the people with real wealth? They weren't braver than you. They were just earlier.

But you? You're here. You're reading. You're building.

And that means fear doesn't run you anymore.

> *"The only thing we have to fear is fear itself"* - Franklin D. Roosevelt

> *"The key to making money with stocks is not to get scared out of them."* – Peter Lynch

> *"The time to buy is when there's blood in the streets."* — Nathan Rothschild

> *"Be greedy when others are fearful, and fearful when others are greedy."* — Warren Buffett

> *"If you scared, go to church"* - O'Shea Jackson Jr. (Ice Cube)

# CHAPTER 8

# YOU'RE THE ASSET: OPTIMIZE YOUR LIFE

The market isn't your biggest investment. **You are**.

Stocks will rise and fall. Companies will come and go. But your skills, your mindset, and your network? That's your real portfolio—and the one you have the most control over.

This chapter is about shifting the spotlight back onto the person reading this book. Because no matter how much money you put into the market—if your life habits are trash, your returns will be too.

## Your Habits Print Money—or Hemorrhage It

Before you think about flipping a stock, ask yourself: what's my daily ROI?

- Do you waste hours on your phone but never study a company?
- Do you spend more on fast food than you invest in your health?
- Do you know more about celebrities than your own credit score?

This isn't shade. This is strategy.

**You are the first business you will ever run**. And every day, you're printing either profit or loss through your habits, decisions, and disciplines.

Everybody knows a bro—hell, *you might even be that bro*—who stays dripped in designer, always in new kicks and fresh fits, but is constantly asking to be Cash App'd a few dollars and never pays it back. And when you finally ask for it? *"My Cash App tweakin' right now... I got you tho!"*

Or the bro who smokes all day—always has weed but never has work. Or maybe the one with 15 baby mamas, who can't make time for his own kids but still finds time to play stepdad to someone else's.

These are all investments, my dear bro. Just poor ones.

The good book says, *"You shall know them by their fruits."*
I'm not here to preach, but the math is universal: **garbage in, garbage out**.
If you spend your time doing bullshit, don't be surprised when your life is filled with bullshit.

*Translation*: *stop doing bullshit. Get off your ass. And start building.*

## High-Value Skills > High-Volatility Stocks

If you want exponential returns, build skills:

- Sales
- Public speaking
- Copywriting
- Coding
- Finance
- Leadership

Pick one. These are assets that print for life. They don't crash. They don't get delisted. They don't expire worthless like an option trade you forgot to close. Invest in courses. Read books. Pay for mentorship.

Not because it's trendy—but because when you sharpen your edge, you multiply your earnings everywhere else.

Throughout my life, I've spent **thousands** on resources—courses, seminars, personal development. This isn't a flex. It's a reminder: self-mastery must be an obsession. That doesn't mean go blow hundreds on some influencer's "get rich quick" bootcamp. But your hunger to better yourself? That should be insatiable.

Some people can't fathom paying for real training. I've heard it myself: "*Wait... you gotta PAY to learn that? Sounds like a scam.*" Bro—you pay for everything. You pay to eat. To sleep. To shit. (Rent, utilities, bills.) You paid for college—even if it was through student loans.

You'll run into folks like this. Their *mindset* is the real red flag. They don't believe in hard work. They don't believe in investing. And they damn sure don't believe in themselves. You're different. You're operating on another bandwidth. So don't take advice from people who've settled for less—family or not, friends or not. They won't see the vision because it's not theirs to see.

## Stock Investing ≠ Life Investing

Too many people try to finesse the market before they've finessed their own damn mindset. They want big returns without big character. They want to 10x their portfolio but can't even 2x their discipline. As Tony Montana once said: "*All I have in this world is my balls and my word, and I don't break 'em for nobody.*" But how many times do you break your own word—to yourself?

You say you'll start working out... then don't. You say you'll read more... then binge Netflix instead. You'll give 40 hours a week to someone else's dream—your job—but zero to your own. And then repeat that cycle for years. Why? Because deep down, you don't respect your own goals. You don't believe you're worthy of achieving them. Or maybe it's easier to say you "*lost passion.*"

Cute excuse. But most people lose passion for their job, their relationship, their dreams—and still show up every day. Passion isn't the problem. Discipline is. You can't keep waiting for a feeling. You need to make a decision.

This book is about mindset. Ownership. Trajectory. It's about reclaiming responsibility—for where you are and where you're headed. And it starts when you invest in, and respect, yourself. Because here's the truth: investing isn't just about money. It's about momentum. Alignment. Vision.

So yes—buy stocks. But also:

- Track your goals.

- Watch your circle.

- Build your body.

- Sharpen your mind.

**Because if you build the life... the money will follow.**

**You** are the asset. And this book? Just a reminder to invest accordingly.

> "*I am the master of my fate, I am the captain of my soul.*" - *William Ernest Henley*

> "*Not being able to govern events, I govern myself*" - *Michel de Montaigne*

> "*God, grant me the serenity to accept the things I cannot change, courage to change the things I can, and wisdom to know the difference.*" - *The Serenity Prayer*

## CHAPTER 9

# BREAK THE CHAIN: HOW GENERATIONAL WEALTH BEGINS WITH YOU

This isn't just about you.

It didn't start with you—but it *can* end with you.

You might be the first in your circle to talk about investing, building credit, or stacking assets. But if you do this right? You **won't** be the last.

This chapter is about legacy. Not the one you were handed. The one you're about to create.

## Be the First, Not the Last

Perhaps nobody taught you this. Perhaps you grew up in survival mode, watching people hustle check to check, never catching a break. Moms working two to three jobs trying to put food on the table. Maybe you had to start working or hustling early in order to provide. Perhaps you grew up around government assistance—unemployment, disability, SSI, food stamps.

I'm not talking down on your upbringing. You had to play the cards you were dealt.

And guess what—none of that disqualifies you. That qualifies you to be the one who flips it.

**You can be the first in your family to:**

- Own stock
- Buy property
- Start a business
- Talk wealth over dinner instead of bills

You're not cursed. You're chosen. You're the break in the pattern.

Myself? I was the offspring of a drug-addicted mother and an abusive father. Both floated in and out of my early life. I was raised by my paternal grandparents. Far from perfect, they carried their own trauma—but they were old-school Black folks who believed in family and hard work. They sacrificed so I could live better. They taught me how to grind. I taught myself how to grind smart.

They couldn't give me what they didn't have. But I chose—through sheer force of will—to bet on myself. Every time. I've argued. I've struggled. I've fallen. But I never stopped believing in what I was building. That belief became a flame. And that flame? It became the foundation for everything I've built.

You've got to find your flame. And never let anyone extinguish it.

That's how you break the cycle—not just for you, but for your people.

## Teach Others. Build Culture. Shift Your Bloodline

Wealth isn't just about money—it's about models. When you learn the game, don't just play it. Teach it. Break it down for your little cousins. Send your friends videos. Drop a gem at the cookout. Start convos that shift mindsets.

Expect pushback. Expect doubt. And understand this: *"When dealing with people, remember you are not dealing with creatures of logic, but with creatures bristling with prejudice and motivated by pride and vanity."* — Dale Carnegie.

The resistance isn't about you—it's about *their* fear. *Their* limits. *Their* unhealed trauma. But brother, this is how cycles break: not with ego. Not with flexing. But with teaching. With patience. With new standards.

Your bloodline isn't just DNA—it's data. It's mindset. It's habit. And when you shift those? You shift everything.

## This Book Is the Spark. You're the Torch.

**What you just read was the introduction. You are the movement.** Without you, this book is just words on a page—inert, meaningless. It's *you* who gives it life. You who carries it forward. Who integrates it. Who lives it. Who passes it on.

Let these words permeate your thoughts, your speech, your decisions. Be the walking case study. Be the example that makes others believe. Claim your rightful place in the world. Share this work with someone else. Buy it. Download it. **Steal it if you must.** Because the time for complacency, victimhood, and lack is over.

**The revolution will not be televised.** It will be **metastasized. Spread. Multiplied.** The spark is lit. **Now burn bright.**

*"He who is brave, is free"* - Seneca

## CLOSING
# REFLECTIONS & REMINDERS

You made it to the end — but this isn't the end. It's the beginning of ownership, alignment, and power. Before you go, let a few thoughts settle in. Not just mine, but the words of people who've walked the walk, built empires, shaped culture, and defied the odds. These are your new mantras. Your reminders. Your fuel.

*"Grind hard, stack your money, and stay out of the way." — Nipsey Hussle*

*"Wealth is not about having money. It's about having options." — Chris Rock*

*"Someone is sitting in the shade today because someone planted a tree a long time ago." — Warren Buffett*

*"Formal education will make you a living; self-education will make you a fortune." — Jim Rohn*

*"Don't work for money. Make money work for you." — Robert Kiyosaki*

*"An investment in knowledge pays the best interest." — Benjamin Franklin*

*"Start where you are. Use what you have. Do what you can." — Arthur Ashe*

*"Believe you can and you're halfway there."* — Theodore Roosevelt

*"Until the lion learns how to write, every story will glorify the hunter."* — African Proverb

*"Get rich or die tryin'."* — 50 Cent

*"Success is not to be pursued; it is to be attracted by the person you become."* — Jim Rohn

*"Opportunities come infrequently. When it rains gold, put out the bucket, not the thimble."* — Warren Buffett

*"If you're born poor, it's not your fault. But if you die poor, it's your fault."* — Bill Gates

*"Your network is your net worth."* — Porter Gale

*"If you want to go fast, go alone. If you want to go far, go together."* — African Proverb

*"The only limit to our realization of tomorrow is our doubts of today."* — Franklin D. Roosevelt

*"Discipline is choosing between what you want now and what you want most."* — Abraham Lincoln

*"The secret of getting ahead is getting started."* — Mark Twain

*"You miss 100% of the shots you don't take."* — Wayne Gretzky

*"Money is a terrible master but an excellent servant."* — P.T. Barnum

You've got the knowledge now. The only question is — will you apply it?

The market doesn't care where you came from. It only cares how you play the game.

Get back in the arena. Stay sharp. Stay dangerous.

And never forget:

They can't stop what they don't understand.

# TERMS THAT MATTER

**Arbitrage** – Taking advantage of price differences in different markets to make a risk-free profit. More advanced play, but worth knowing.

**Asset** – Anything that has value and can generate cash flow or grow in value.

**Asset Allocation** – The process of spreading your investments across different asset types (like stocks, bonds, real estate) to balance risk and reward.

**Ask Price** – The lowest price a seller is willing to accept for an asset.

**Bear Market** – A market condition where prices are falling, typically by 20% or more from recent highs, and investor sentiment is pessimistic.

**Bid Price** – The highest price a buyer is willing to pay for an asset.

**Blue Chip Stock** – Shares of large, reputable, and financially sound companies with a history of stable performance (e.g., Apple, Microsoft).

**Bond** – A loan you give to a company or government in exchange for regular interest payments and the return of the bond's face value when it matures.

**Broker** – The platform you use to buy and sell investments (e.g., Robinhood, Fidelity).

**Bull Market** – A market condition where prices are generally rising, driven by optimism and investor confidence.

**Capital** – Money used to invest or start a business; financial resources available for use.

**Capital Gains** – Profit made from selling an asset for more than you bought it.

**Compounding Interest** – When the interest you earn starts earning its own interest—growth on growth.

**Credit** – The ability to borrow money with the promise to pay it back later, usually with interest.

**Debt** – Money you owe to someone else.

**Debit** – Money withdrawn directly from your available funds.

**Diversification** – Spreading your investments across different assets to reduce risk.

**Dividend** – A payout from a company to its shareholders, usually from profits.

**Dollar Cost Averaging** – Investing a fixed amount of money on a regular schedule regardless of market conditions.

**Economy** – The overall system of how money flows through production, consumption, labor, and trade in a country.

**Earnings** – The profits a company makes, usually reported quarterly. Strong earnings can push a stock higher; weak earnings can tank it. Pay attention—earnings tell the story behind the stock price.

**ETF (Exchange-Traded Fund)** – A basket of stocks that trades like a single stock.

**Expense Ratio** – The percentage of your investment a fund charges annually to manage the assets. It's taken out automatically—you're not paying it separately—but it slightly reduces your returns over time.

**Ex-Dividend Date** – The cutoff date to be eligible to receive a stock's next dividend. Buy before this date if you want that payout.

**GDP (Gross Domestic Product)** – The total value of all goods and services produced in a country during a specific time period.

**Index Fund** – A type of mutual fund or ETF designed to track a specific segment of the market (like the S&P 500).

**Inflation** – The rate at which the general level of prices for goods and services is rising, reducing purchasing power.

**Interest** – The cost of borrowing money or the return you get from lending it or investing it.

**Leverage** – Using borrowed capital to increase potential returns (or losses) on an investment.

**Limit Buy** – A type of order to purchase a security at or below a specific price, allowing you to control how much you're willing to pay.

**Liquidity** – How quickly and easily you can access or convert your money.

**Margin** – Borrowed money from your broker that lets you buy more stock than you could with just your cash. It can magnify gains—but it can also magnify losses. Use with caution. Margin ain't free—it comes with interest.

**Market Cap (Capitalization)** – The total value of a company's outstanding shares of stock.

**Options** – Contracts that give you the right (but not the obligation) to buy or sell an asset at a certain price within a certain time frame.

**P/E Ratio (Price-to-Earnings Ratio)** – A way to measure how expensive or cheap a stock is relative to its earnings. A basic tool to check if a stock looks overhyped or undervalued.

**Portfolio** – Your collection of investments.

**Resistance Level** – A price point where a stock tends to stop rising because selling increases. Traders watch resistance to spot potential sell zones.

**Return on Investment (ROI)** – The percentage of profit or loss you make on an investment compared to what you originally put in. It measures how effectively your money is working for you.

**Risk Tolerance** – How comfortable you are with the possibility of losing money in pursuit of gains.

**Sector** – A group of companies that operate in the same industry (e.g., tech, healthcare, energy).

**Stock** – A share of ownership in a company.

**Stop-Loss** – A pre-set order to sell a stock if it drops to a certain price to limit your loss.

**Support Level** – A price point where a stock tends to stop falling because demand increases. Traders watch support to spot potential buy zones.

**Time Horizon** – The length of time you plan to hold an investment before taking the money out.

**Trade** – The act of buying or selling a financial asset.

**Treasury** – Government-issued debt securities (like T-bills, notes, and bonds) used to fund public spending.

**VIX (Volatility Index)** – A measure of market volatility—known as the "fear gauge." Higher VIX = more market fear and bigger price swings.

**Volatility** – How much the price of a stock or asset moves up and down.

**Yield** – The income return on an investment, often shown as a percentage.

# WANNA GO DEEPER??

You know the basics now. You've learned how to move with purpose, how to invest smart, and how to think long term. But maybe you want more. Maybe you want to learn how to read a chart, flip a trade, and pull profit in a day—or even in an hour.

If that's you? You're ready for Book 2: *Aye Bro, You Tryna Trade Forreal?*
This one ain't for the dabblers.
It's for the ones who want precision.

We're talking:

- Options
- Futures
- Chart patterns
- Trader psychology
- Risk management

It's where we break down high-level trading with low-key explanations.

If investing is the marathon, trading is the sprint.

You ready to train?

# | ACKNOWLEDGMENTS

First, to myself—for the obvious reasons. The late nights, the deep dives, the discipline. You kept going. Even when the universe itself seemed against you, you preserved. Now look at you, building something greater than anyone had imagined. You are the pride of your family, you are the prayer of your ancestors, you are the embodiment of success on every quantifiable level.

To my son—my living legacy. Before you, I was building for myself. Now, every move I make is done with you in mind. Looking at you forces me to elevate. This book is part blueprint, part offering. So one day, when you ask what a boss looks like—I can just point to the mirror. You will never know what it feels like to be unloved or unsupported. I want to be someone you can be proud of; and should I live long enough to see you as a man, I want to see you as someone I can be proud of too.

To my readers and supporters—you didn't have to believe in me, but you did. Your feedback, your reposts, your energy—it fuels the mission. I never imagined this would resonate the way it has. You turned pages into a movement. My only wish is for you to elevate yourself and pass it on. Without "common-unity" there is no community. The day we all get on the same accord is the day *they fear* the most. I've done my part. The rest is on you.

To the fallen soldiers who left their mark:

- *Tae M.* — Your fearless spirit still echoes. You never followed—you led. A real one. A visionary. A businessman before the world caught on. Your ambition was inspiring, and I only wish I had told you that when we were kids. You were going to make it out, bro. I know it. You lived on your terms, and I know you wouldn't have had it any other way.

- *Brandon J.* — My brother in security. If only you knew how much you mattered. From riding together, working together, to standing ten toes together—people knew to stay in line when we showed up. I wish I had been more open, more understanding. Maybe it would've made a difference. You deserved better.

- *Curtis L.* — Our time was short, but your impact was real. You made sure I was straight from day one, dropped gems on how to level up, and inspired me to think bigger. When you saw me work that stick, you said it made you want to grab your own. If only you got the chance to use it. You lived fully, brother—just wish you had more time.

To everyone who doubted me, who crossed me, who played villain in my story—you added gasoline to the fire. Your negativity, your spite, your shade? Transmuted. You helped forge this version of me. Stronger. Sharper. Hungrier. So thank you. I couldn't have done it without you.

And to you, reading this now—may you reap all the success you deserve.

# END

www.ingramcontent.com/pod-product-compliance
Lightning Source LLC
Chambersburg PA
CBHW071240090426
42736CB00014B/3152